I Have the Flu

Gillian Gosman

PowerKiDS press
New York

Published in 2013 by The Rosen Publishing Group, Inc.
29 East 21st Street, New York, NY 10010

Copyright © 2013 by The Rosen Publishing Group, Inc.

All rights reserved. No part of this book may be reproduced in any form without permission in writing from the publisher, except by a reviewer.

First Edition

Editor: Jennifer Way
Book Design: Greg Tucker
Layout Design: Kate Laczynski

Photo Credits: Cover, pp. 8, 10, 13, 20, 22 Shutterstock.com; pp. 4–5 George Doyle/Stockbyte/Thinkstock; p. 6 Dorling Kindersley/the Agency Collection/Getty Images; p. 7 Michael Krasowitz/Photographer's Choice/Getty Images; p. 9 (top) NYPL/Science Source/Photo Researchers/Getty Images; p. 9 (bottom) NIBSC/Science Photo Library/Getty Images; p. 11 Kin Images/Riser/Getty Images; p. 12 Buena Vista Images/Lifesize/Getty Images; p 14 BananaStock/Thinkstock; p. 15 (top) © www.iStockphoto.com/Maartje van Caspel; p. 15 (bottom) © www.iStockphoto.com/Stefanie Timmermann; pp. 16–17 Stockbyte/Thinkstock; p. 18 Hemera/Thinkstock; p. 19 (top) © www.iStockphoto.com/EdStock; pp. 19 (bottom), 21 © www.iStockphoto.com/Kim Gunkel.

Library of Congress Cataloging-in-Publication Data

Gosman, Gillian.
 I have the flu / by Gillian Gosman. — 1st ed.
    p. cm. — (Get well soon!)
 Includes index.
 ISBN 978-1-4488-7409-5 (library binding)
 1. Influenza—Juvenile literature. I. Title.

RC150.G67 2013
616.2'03—dc23

2011047814

Manufactured in the United States of America

CPSIA Compliance Information: Batch #SW12PK: For Further Information contact Rosen Publishing, New York, New York at 1-800-237-9932

Contents

I Have the Flu	4
What Is the Flu?	6
Which Flu Is It?	8
Signs and Symptoms	10
What's Going On in My Body?	12
How Did I Catch the Flu?	14
Going to the Doctor	16
How the Flu Is Treated	18
How to Prevent the Flu	20
The Road to Recovery	22
Glossary	23
Index	24
Websites	24

I Have the Flu

Every fall, people get ready for what is called the winter flu season. The flu can make your body ache, your head hurt, and your stomach feel queasy. It leaves you with a fever, chills, and sometimes even a bad case of dizziness!

Each year, more than 100 million Americans get the flu **vaccine**, in the hope of avoiding the misery of the flu. The vaccine is given in a shot. The flu shot is meant to protect you from getting the flu. People who got the vaccine last year are not totally safe from catching the flu this year, though. That is because the **virus** that causes the flu changes every year!

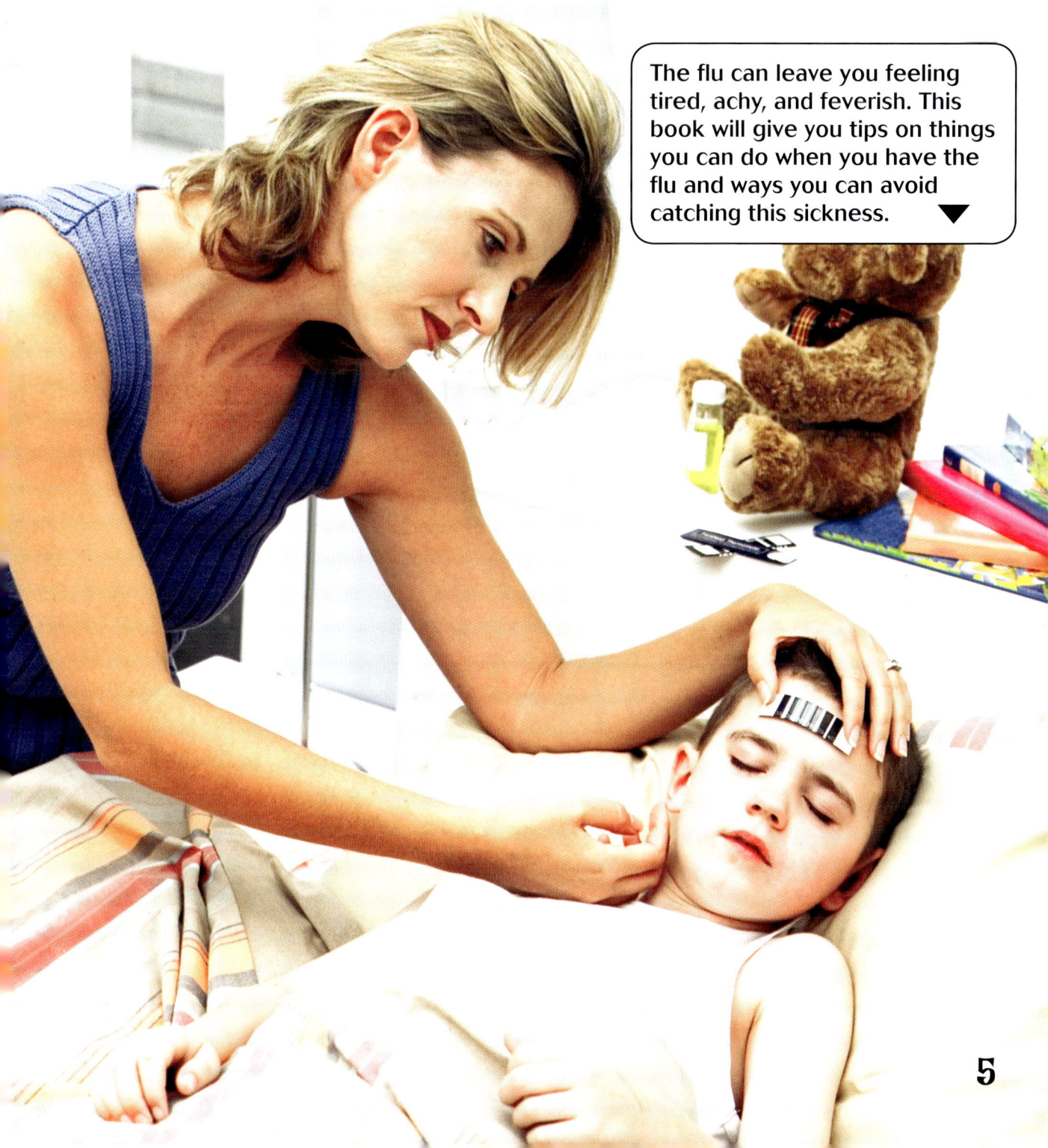

The flu can leave you feeling tired, achy, and feverish. This book will give you tips on things you can do when you have the flu and ways you can avoid catching this sickness. ▼

What Is the Flu?

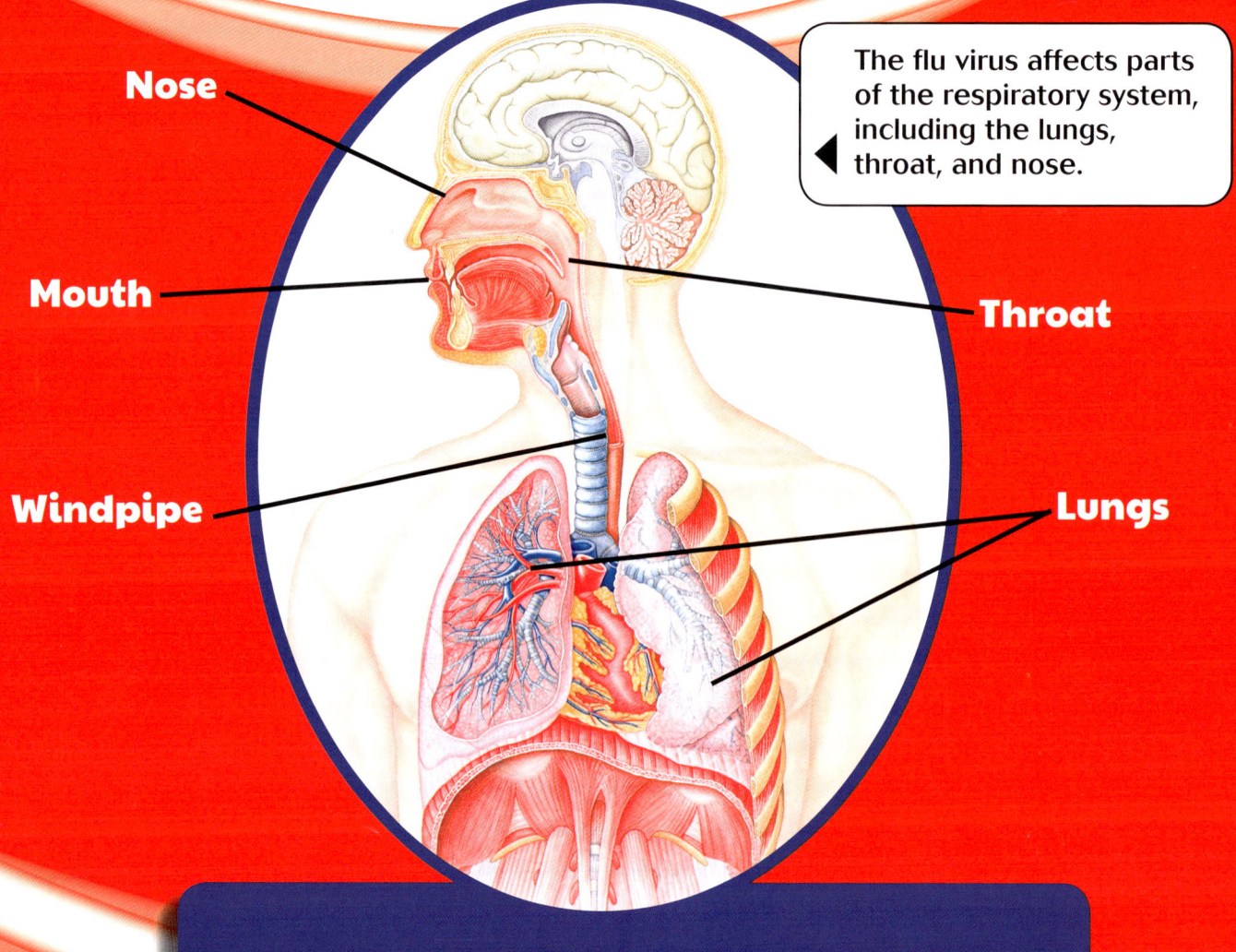

- Nose
- Mouth
- Windpipe
- Throat
- Lungs

The flu virus affects parts of the respiratory system, including the lungs, throat, and nose.

The flu is an **infection** of the **respiratory system**. This body system includes the passageways of the throat and nose.

When you have a respiratory infection like the flu, you often have a cough and a stuffy head. The fever that this infection brings can cause other signs and symptoms, such as headaches and body aches.

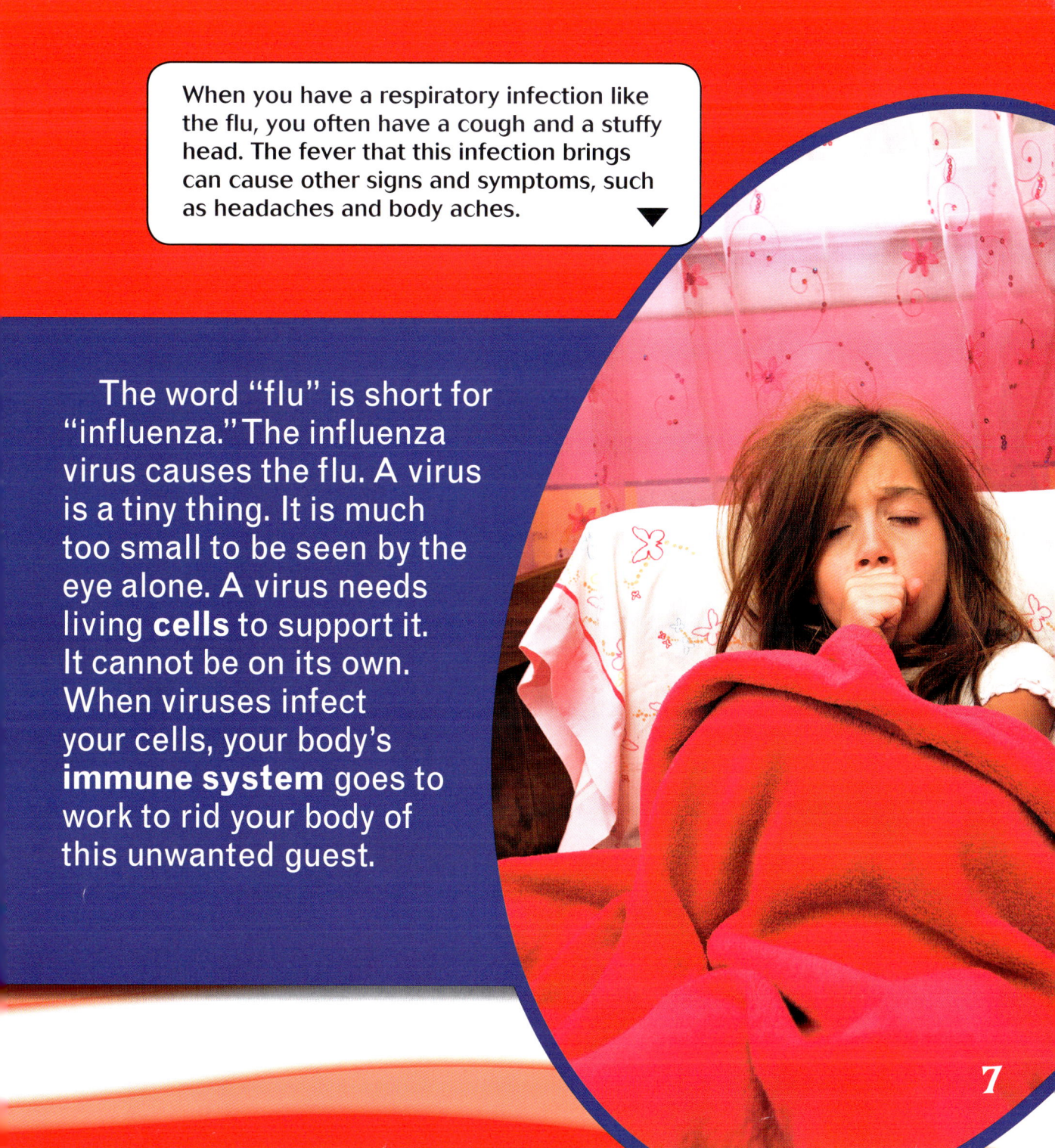

The word "flu" is short for "influenza." The influenza virus causes the flu. A virus is a tiny thing. It is much too small to be seen by the eye alone. A virus needs living **cells** to support it. It cannot be on its own. When viruses infect your cells, your body's **immune system** goes to work to rid your body of this unwanted guest.

Which Flu Is It?

There are several strains, or kinds, of influenza viruses. Most kinds of influenza viruses can be treated with rest and medicine. The people most likely to become seriously sick from the flu are children, the elderly, and people who have health problems like heart disease or asthma.

Illnesses like the flu spread easily at schools. It is easy to spread germs in places where lots of people gather and share food, drinks, toys, and school supplies.

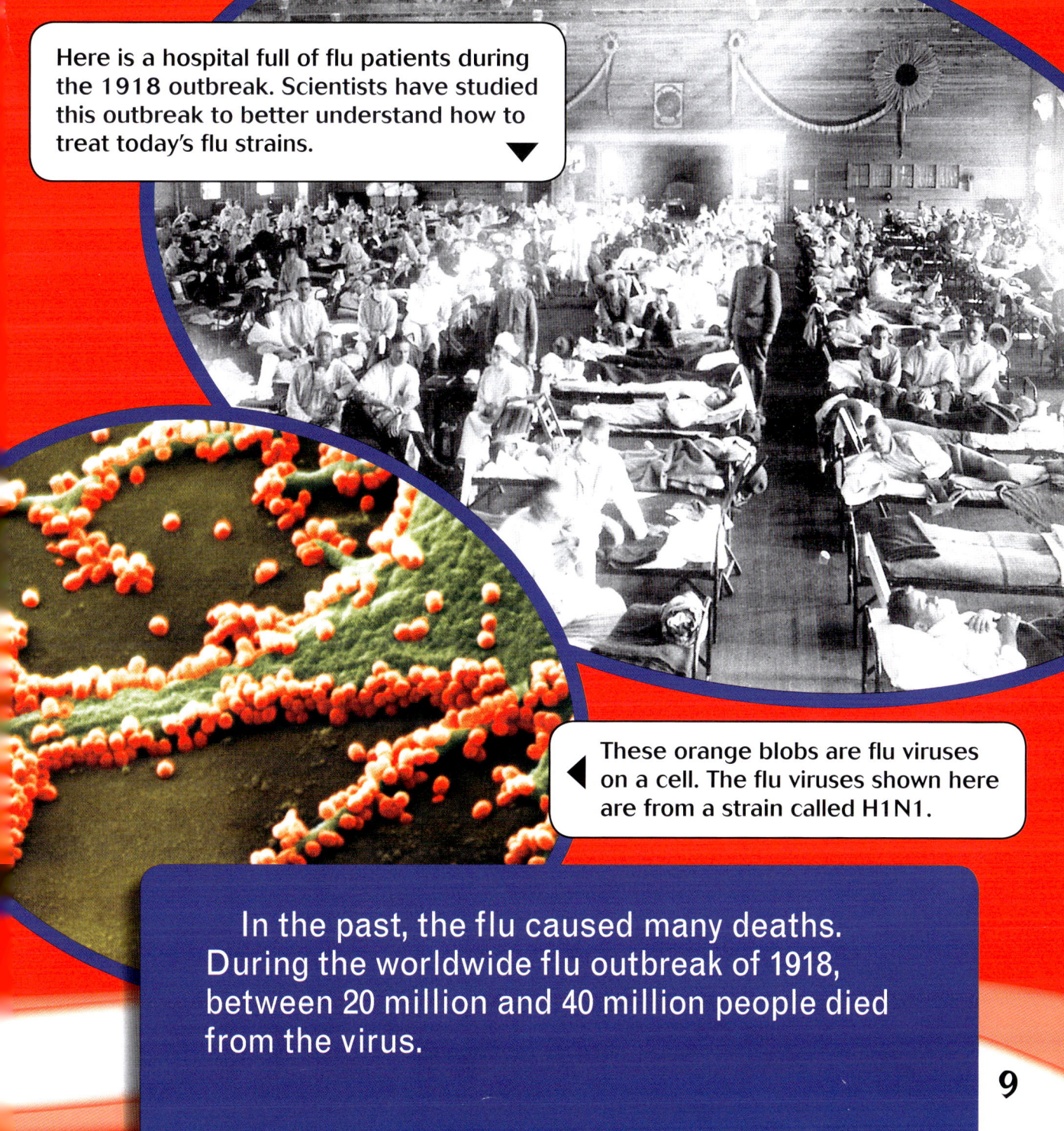

Here is a hospital full of flu patients during the 1918 outbreak. Scientists have studied this outbreak to better understand how to treat today's flu strains.

These orange blobs are flu viruses on a cell. The flu viruses shown here are from a strain called H1N1.

In the past, the flu caused many deaths. During the worldwide flu outbreak of 1918, between 20 million and 40 million people died from the virus.

Signs and Symptoms

Most people who get the flu will have several common **signs** and **symptoms**. A sign is a medical term that describes information a doctor can observe in a patient or check using medical tools. A symptom is a medical term that describes what a patient tells a doctor about what she feels.

▲
When you have a fever, your head may feel hot to the touch. Your parent or a doctor may take your temperature with a thermometer to measure this sign, though.

A dry cough and sleepiness are two classic symptoms of the flu.

In patients with the flu, doctors may note a fever of 100.4° F (38° C) or higher. Patients complain of a dry cough, sore throat, runny nose, sleepiness, and body aches. Some patients might even vomit or have **diarrhea**. These signs and symptoms add up to a patient who feels terrible!

What's Going On in My Body?

When a flu virus enters your body, it finds a healthy cell. The virus forces this host cell to create copies of the flu virus. The virus is copied again and again inside the cell until the host cell bursts. The virus then spreads to other healthy cells.

As the infection spreads, your immune system starts to fight

◀ The mucus your body makes when you are sick helps trap and get rid of the flu virus. To keep from spreading these germs, throw away used tissues and wash your hands often.

back. It sends cells whose job it is to destroy the virus. This can cause **inflammation**, which you experience as a fever. Your immune system also makes a lot of clear, watery **mucus** to trap the virus. This mucus drips from your nose and runs down your throat.

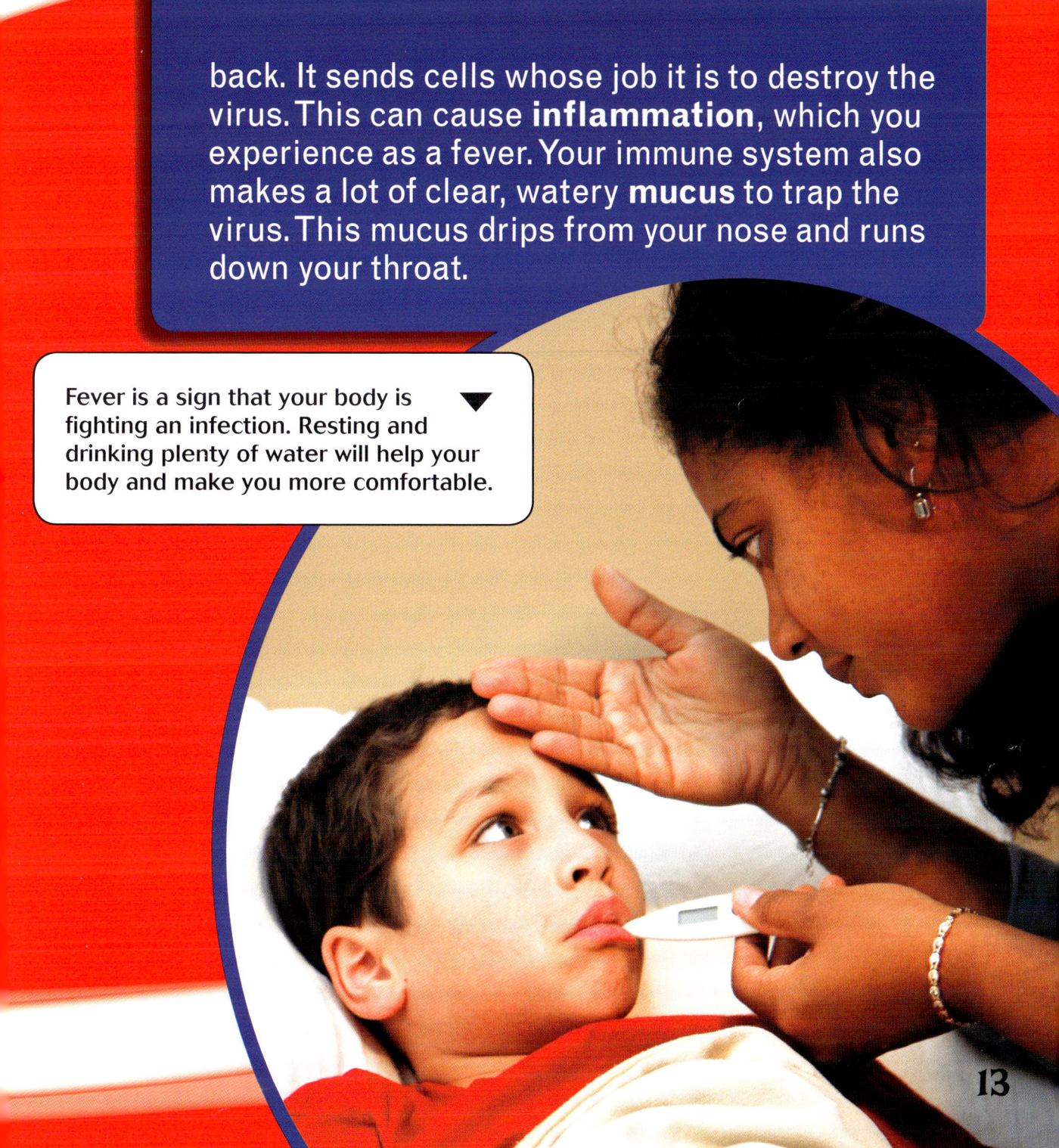

Fever is a sign that your body is fighting an infection. Resting and drinking plenty of water will help your body and make you more comfortable.

How Did I Catch the Flu?

Flu viruses travel through the air in tiny drops of mucus. When a sick person coughs or sneezes, this mucus leaves his body and flies in every direction. It is important to cover your nose and mouth with your arm or a tissue when you cough or sneeze. This will help keep germs from spreading in this way.

A sneeze can leave your body at up to 93 miles per hour (150 km/h)! If your nose and mouth are not covered, that sneeze blasts germs out into the air.

When there is a big flu outbreak, some people wear masks over their noses and mouths. They hope this will keep them from picking up the flu virus when they are in crowded places. ▶

Cough or sneeze into your arm. This keeps germs from spreading into the air and keeps germs off of your hands. ◀

If a healthy person breathes in these tiny drops of mucus or if she touches a hard surface where mucus has landed and then touches her eyes, nose, or mouth, she could pick up the virus. The signs and symptoms of the flu start to appear soon after.

Going to the Doctor

Doctors do not think all patients with the flu need to visit a doctor or nurse. This is because most cases of the flu are not very serious. However, young children, older adults, and people with some health problems should visit the doctor right away.

Usually, the signs and symptoms of the flu are clear. There is also a quick and easy test for the flu. The doctor swabs the nose or throat. This is done by rubbing a small piece of cotton across the inside of these surfaces. This piece of cotton is then tested for the flu virus.

▲
If you have a fever that lasts longer than three days, you should see a doctor.

17

How the Flu Is Treated

Any time your body's immune system is fighting an infection, it helps to drink plenty of water. Making sure to get plenty of rest is important, too. Your doctor might tell you to take an over-the-counter children's painkiller. This medicine will help lower your fever and ease the pain in your muscles.

It is also important to try not to go out in crowded public places. The flu is

◀ Your parent might give you an over-the-counter medicine for your flu symptoms. This will help you with your aches and fever.

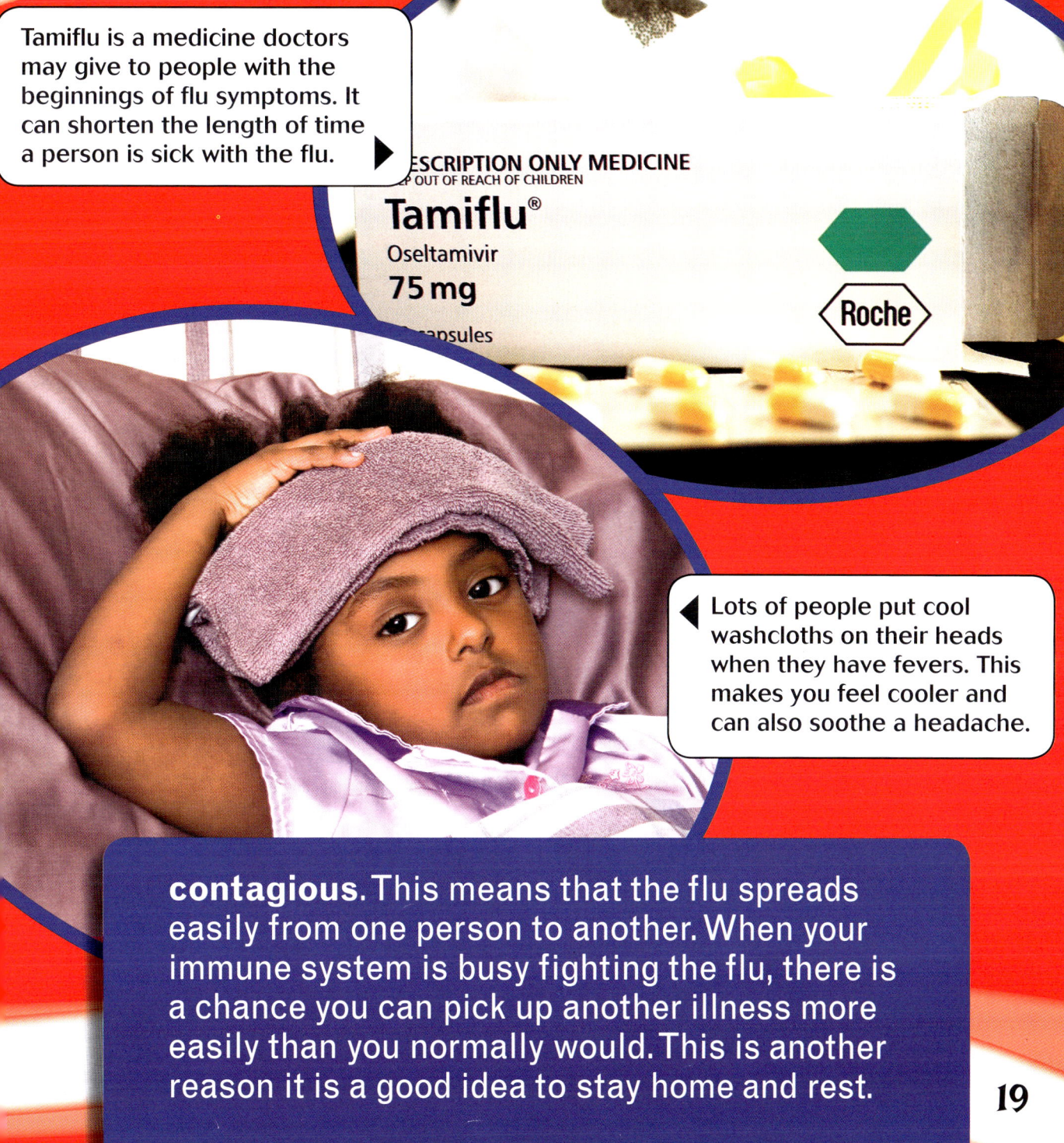

Tamiflu is a medicine doctors may give to people with the beginnings of flu symptoms. It can shorten the length of time a person is sick with the flu.

Lots of people put cool washcloths on their heads when they have fevers. This makes you feel cooler and can also soothe a headache.

contagious. This means that the flu spreads easily from one person to another. When your immune system is busy fighting the flu, there is a chance you can pick up another illness more easily than you normally would. This is another reason it is a good idea to stay home and rest.

How to Prevent the Flu

The flu spreads from one person to the next, so the best way to avoid getting sick is to stay away from people who have the flu. This is not always possible, though. To be on the safe side, wash your hands often, and do not share food and drinks with others. Cleaning surfaces with **disinfecting** spray or wipes kills germs on counters, doorknobs, and other places where you could pick up the flu.

◄ Vaccines are an important part of stopping the spread of certain illnesses. That is why it is recommended that people get flu shots every year.

Doctors now recommend that most people get flu shots every autumn. The flu vaccine changes every year to protect people against new strains of the virus. This helps stop the spread of the flu, too.

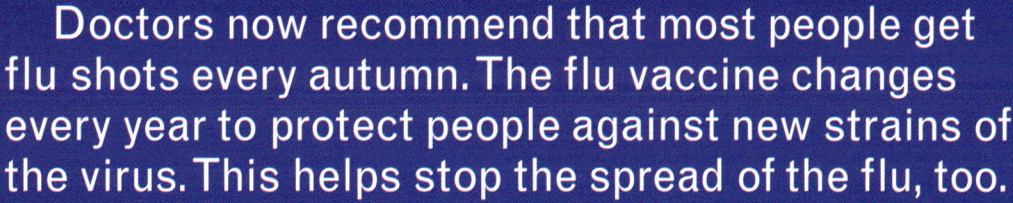

Washing your hands with soap and warm water helps remove the flu virus and other germs from your hands.

21

The Road to Recovery

> The worst part of the flu usually passes after a few days. It may take another week before you are back to your healthy self, but you are on the road to recovery.

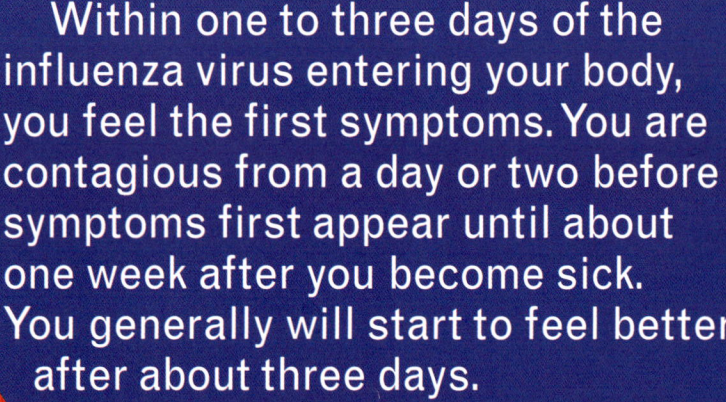

Within one to three days of the influenza virus entering your body, you feel the first symptoms. You are contagious from a day or two before symptoms first appear until about one week after you become sick. You generally will start to feel better after about three days.

If the patient does not rest and recover, the flu can lead to more serious sicknesses. These might include pneumonia or ear infections. The flu can also make other health problems worse. Patients with diabetes, asthma, or heart disease must be very careful to take care of themselves so they can get well quickly.

Glossary

cells (SELZ) The basic units of living things.

contagious (kun-TAY-jus) Can be passed on.

diarrhea (dy-uh-REE-uh) Having very watery stools and having to go very often.

disinfecting (dis-in-FEKT-ing) Making something clean and free of things that can make people sick.

immune system (ih-MYOON SIS-tem) The system that keeps the body safe from sicknesses.

infection (in-FEK-shun) A sickness caused by germs.

inflammation (in-fluh-MAY-shun) Something that is sore or swollen.

mucus (MYOO-kus) Thick, slimy matter produced by the body.

respiratory system (RES-puh-ruh-tawr-ee SIS-tem) The parts of the body that help in breathing.

signs (SYNZ) Things that show that one might have an illness.

symptoms (SIMP-tumz) Information patients give doctors about illnesses based on what they are feeling.

vaccine (vak-SEEN) A shot that keeps a person from getting a certain sickness.

virus (VY-rus) Something tiny that causes a disease.

Index

A
Americans, 4, 8

B
body, 4, 7, 12, 14, 22

C
cell(s), 7, 12–13
chills, 4

D
diarrhea, 11
dizziness, 4

F
fever, 4, 11, 13, 18

H
head, 4

I
immune system, 7, 12–13, 18–19
infection(s), 6, 12, 18, 22
inflammation, 13

M
mucus, 13–15

P
passageways, 6
people, 4, 8–10, 16, 20–21

R
respiratory system, 6

S
season, 4
shot(s), 4, 21
stomach, 4
surface(s), 15–16, 20

T
throat, 6, 11, 13, 16

V
vaccine, 4, 21
virus(es), 4, 7–9, 12–16, 21–22

Websites

Due to the changing nature of Internet links, PowerKids Press has developed an online list of websites related to the subject of this book. This site is updated regularly. Please use this link to access the list: www.powerkidslinks.com/gws/flu/